CONTENT

INTRODUCTION

Hi, my name is Adeline. For the first seven to eight years of my professional career as a magician, I worked as a kids and family birthday party magician, and was known as Kinetic Gal. Through those years, I worked on not just the birthday party magic, but also on theming and helping parents organize a stress free birthday party.

I was lucky enough to have helped hundreds of children celebrate their birthdays, and fortunate enough to have the local media identify me as one of the top birthday party entertainers in Singapore. Throughout those years, I maintained a blog with articles on ideas, tips and cheat sheets for a stress free birthday party. Having moved on to corporate performances, the blog is now defunct. However, I would like to share the tips and ideas that were borne out of the experience I had throughout the eight years. This book is based on that, and I hope you find information useful for you.

A birthday party is the celebration of the birth of the jewel of your life, and should not be stressful! It should be fun... for both your child and you.

Here is to an awesome celebration!

Adeline Ng

PLANNING THE BIRTHDAY PARTY – START EARLY

Many people leave the planning of the birthday party till it is just around the corner. That really only makes the stress a lot more that it should be!

As a rough guideline, the time to start to plan the birthday party should be from 1.5 months – 2months before. The sourcing of a venue should start from about 2 months before. In the Singapore context, many a times, parents conduct the birthday party in the community function room (which can only be booked a month in advance). In such cases, an alternative venue should be kept in mind just in case.

If professional entertainment is preferred, then the booking should be about 1.5 months before the party as the good entertainers get booked early.

This timeline also allows time for purchase of DIY materials should a DIY party be preferred.

So what exactly should the timing be like to organize your party? Here's a basic timeline!

THE PARTY ORGANIZATION TIMELINE!

2 MONTHS BEFORE: Start searching for a suitable party entertainer/ party host.

1.5 MONTHS BEFORE: Settle on party entertainer/ party host + decorations + preliminary date for party.

1 MONTH BEFORE: Confirm party date and look for food caterer (if you are having food catering).

3 WEEKS BEFORE: Send out party invites. Also, purchase of materials for party (DIY or decorations etc.)

2 WEEKS BEFORE: RSVP invitations and confirm caterer (and party bags if it is not included in entertainment package).

1 WEEK BEFORE: Look for birthday cake and order in advance.

2 DAYS BEFORE: RSVP invitations again and prepare snacks etc.

PARTY TIME! Enjoy yourselves!

1 DAY AFTER: Relax and give yourself a huge pat on the back for a party brilliantly planned.

[Optional] 1 week after: Start thinking of a new theme for your next party!

That really, is a recommended timeline in brief. Of course, you could also, simply just give a call to a professional party entertainment company to settle the food, decorations and party bags for you, leaving you the easy and simple organization for party invites and cake!

Whatever it is, remember to plan in advance so you will have ample time to look around for the best, and not be too tired out by the whole process. After all, the essence of having a party is to relax and have fun!

INVOLVING THE CHILD

Personally, I am a huge advocate of involving the child in the birthday party planning. It is a great chance to do some parent-child bonding.

Through the selection and involvement process, you may learn some surprising things about your child. In my years of hosting birthday parties, parents have shared interesting anecdotes about uncovering something that they never knew about their kid.

J is a friend of mine, and a professional ventriloquist based in Singapore. One day, we were exchanging stories, and he shared about a party he hosted. It turned out that the birthday child was extremely afraid of his puppets! Because the child was not involved in the planning, the parents had no idea! Luckily, J was a pro and could entertain the children with games, song and dances. WHEW!

In any case, the birthday party is a celebration of the child's birthday. Unless it is meant as a surprise, the child might like to be able to discuss the theming.

DATE SELECTION

In general, weekends are favoured for parties.

The date selection might be a different process however if the birthday party falls during the school holiday seasons. Many parents are surprised to find out that if the child's birthday falls during the school holiday season, the turnout for the birthday party might be quite low.

This is mostly due to the fact that nowadays many parents take their children overseas for the holiday. In fact, it is a known fact to kids and family entertainers that birthday party bookings are usually lowest during the holiday season (we work the malls during those season instead). As such, it might be prudent to check with the other parents (especially of the BFFs of your child!). I have come across a good number of situations where the birthday party was brought forward by 2 weeks or even more to accommodate the child's BFFs.

TIME SELECTION

It might come as a surprise that timing comes into play for a party. For most children above the age of 4, general evening or afternoon timing works for parties. However, for children aged 4 and below, do take into consideration the child's nap time!

Many a times, I have hosted parties where the birthday child is exceptionally cranky because he or she has not had the afternoon nap!

VENUE SELECTION

In Singapore, a popular venue to host the birthday party is actually... in the childcare centre. Yup! Most childcare centres allow for birthday parties to be hosted in the centre. However, most times, when parties are hosted in child care centres, there are rules and regulations.

Some things to note about childcare centres:

- Many do not allow animals (for fear of allergy).
- Some do not allow home prepared food (eg. MacDonald's and pre-packed food and beverages are fine, but home-prepped sandwiches may not be allowed)
- Time limit and restrictions. Most child care centres have regulated timing for nap time and tea time, so the timing of the party works around the time table. Most allotted timing do not exceed 1.5 hours (including food/ tea-time).

Other venue ideas:

- Function Rooms (Condominiums/ Hotel)
- Play Gyms
- BBQ/ Beaches (tough to conduct a birthday party for younger kids)
- Poolside (safety paramount)
- Home
- Anywhere with a decent space

Where are some of the places to hold a good birthday party? Sometimes, parents do come up to us after shows, asking about some suggestions, so here we have some suggestions from the wacky mind of

Kinetic Gal! (Don't worry though, the suggestions are very much sane!)

Here I have some suggestions that you can consider, with the pros and cons listed, as well as some things to look out for. The list is not comprehensive enough since I only list basic birthday party locations.

1. Home!

If your house is big enough, why not consider having it there and then in your home?

Pros: Easy for arrangement and of course, it is a familiar environment!

Cons: Cleaning up may not be that easy!

Things to note: Do try to figure out in advance where the food, entertainment and games area should be. As far as possible, they should be separate so that kids won't be knocking into adults holding food and etc.

2. Function Room (either of your estate, or a relative/friends' estate)

Pros: Relatively big area to work with, rates are cheap and you get a good nice area to set up.

Cons: Time restrictive and again, you do have to pack up the area!

Things to note: Nothing much really, unless the rooms are near to houses, then you might want to note that you will have to control your noise level!

3. Restaurants

Pros: You get food in one area, and there is no need to clean up!

Cons: Not much entertainment going on for the kids! You also have to ensure restaurant has a stage if you wish to hire an entertainer or no one would be able to see anything!

Things to note: More suitable for older kids. Younger kids appreciate having space to run around, restaurant setting may be just a tad too restrained. Look also for a more family oriented restaurants! They are more likely to be able to accede to your requests and the things you need.

** Certain restaurants (like Hard Rock Cafe) actually have a separate room that may be able to be booked for birthday parties. If so, these are actually ideal as they have a less formal setting, and more likely than not, a space that is specially catered for the entertainers!

4. Country Clubs

Pros: Good, family centred clubs are great in this aspect! Most people do expect parties to be going on and kids allowed quite a free run around the area as long as no one knocks into stuff. Most of stage (or staging can be provided) so you can be assured that the entertainers have got a good spot to perform. You can arrange for club in-house restaurants as well and sometimes you can have packages for these events. Plan it well and it can be even fair-like and a hot talking point amongst your little kids' friends for weeks.

Cons: Higher end clubs can be pretty expensive!

Things to note: Include instructions and maps in your invites! Some clubs are not that accessible and not everyone knows how to reach the place. Also, if it is a high end club, you might want to include dressing information as these clubs will be stricter. You do not want unhappy friends who are turned away due to attiring problems!

5. Chalets

Pros: Fantastic for kids with huge number of friends, and good activities to keep the kids occupied all day long. Throw in a BBQ which everyone loves and it will definitely be a memorable birthday party!

Cons: Extremely hard to arrange space for entertainer to work!

Things to note: Chalets are mostly in the further out regions, so you might expect lower attendance! Otherwise, there might be more kids leaving early and you should be prepared that many kids will be in and out of the place and you may not be able to track everyone. This might be of a concern if kids are still young. Recommended more for kids ages 10 and above.

There are of course some other places still, which include: Kid's gym, swimming pool (take note for this: safety is a huge consideration!), theme parks, zoos, gardens, beaches (again, take note of safety concerns) and many more.

PARTY TYPES

Here are some broad ideas and categories of birthday party types.

- Fun and Show
    - o Magic Shows
    - o Science Shows
    - o Balloon Shows
- Games and Movement
    - o Dance Party
    - o Games Party (Trivia, etc.)
    - o Gym Party
- Story-telling & Dress-up
- Experiential
    - o Workshop based
    - o Fun Tour
- Activity-based
    - o Laser Tag
    - o Football
    - o Rock-climbing

Depending on your child's personality and the amount of time you are able to spend on the organisation, you will find yourself being partial to several. Some of the party types are more "hands-free" or dependent on professional entertainers, while the others can be more involved.

Usually, there is also a mix of party-types. For example, many times, show type parties are mixed with movement and games. Since children are naturally active, so mixing up the party can enhance their fun-catching and prevent boredom.

PLANNING THE PARTY SCHEDULE

Many parents face the difficulty of choosing the time for the entertainer/party host to come in to do a show. Here are some guidelines as to how to plan the timing for the party:

The timing for the entertainment depends on the various considerations you do. You would have to consider the guests (age of the kids), the food to be provided (if you are providing any), whether it is a school day the next day, the length of time of the entertainment and so on and so forth.

First and foremost, it is a no brainer that you should first decide whether you will be providing lunch or tea or dinner for the party. Deciding on this aspect gives you general timeframe to work within and plan accordingly. Assuming you have decided on providing a buffet dinner, the next thing you would want to ask yourself is if you wish for your guest to have entertainment and cake-cutting before dinner or after dinner.

If you wish for entertainment to come before your dinner, do remember to indicate on your invitation card that you have hired entertainment for the party before the dinner. This ensures that your guests will come in on time, and not miss the entertainment planned for them. It would be prudent to check the rough amount of time that the entertainment will be provided for so that your guests will not be starving before the entertainment is over.

If you were to wish for the entertainment to be provided after dinner, remember to indicate that on your invitation card as well. One particular point to note is that, if the average age of the children is younger, this may not be appropriate as they tend to need to sleep early. Also, if it happens to be a school day the next day, parents may not want to allow their kids to stay so late. In that case, it may be wiser to have the entertainment before dinner instead.

This would be more or less the same for lunch with the consideration that young kids tend to need an afternoon nap at around 3 in the afternoon and so, entertainment after lunch should try not to extend beyond that. For parties providing tea (i.e. light refreshments only), you would have a higher flexibility of when to have the entertainment since the children (and guests) would most probably be good with both eating before and after the entertainment.

Time slots of 9am/ 11am/ 1pm/ 3pm/ 5pm/ 7pm/ 9pm work great for parties. These time slots have been given due considerations so you can have your food before/after the party games and entertainment as you have planned. Indeed, having a good planning of the party ensures that you (plus your kid) and the guests would be able to enjoy yourselves to the fullest without starving or having to go off halfway during the show.

IDEAS AND TIPS

DIY PINATAS

Previously, Kinetic Gal (yours truly) wrote about piñatas, and well, in this post, I will be writing about one simple and fun way which you can try to make your own traditional piñata together with your kid. Let us get started!

Materials needed:

- Balloon (+pump)
- Treats and prizes (hard candy that does not melt easily)
- Newspaper
- Starch
- Water

Steps

1. Stuff prizes into the balloon, one by one. (Be careful!)
2. Blow up the balloon carefully, without jiggling the balloon too much – sweets packaging have sharp edges, you do not want the balloons bursting. *Pump is recommended as balloons occasionally burst and can pose a hazard if you're blowing it by mouth*
3. When it has reached a suitable size, tie it up.
4. Mix starch and water in a bowl. Make sure it is starchy enough – just like glue.
5. Tear newspaper in strips and soak them in the starch water.

6. Paste newspaper strips on balloon until sufficiently thick – around 3 to 5 layers. Leave the balloon end (where you blow up the balloon) sticking out. This end is needed later on to suspend the piñata.
7. Set aside to dry fully.
8. Stick a needle in the balloon end to burst the balloon and pull out the balloon bits.
9. Start decorating your piñata by painting on the newspaper.
10. Set to dry – TADAH!

To suspend the piñata, first tie a length of ribbon to the middle of the ice-cream stick. Slip the ice-cream stick vertically into the piñata through the hole. Once it is in, it should lie horizontally and thus will not come out from the inside easily. Tie the ribbon to the ceiling and you are done!

Now all you are left with is to get a bat (be careful!), clear the ancient flower vases out of the way and wait for piñata time.

TREATS

In general, what are some birthday party treats one can prepare for a great birthday party? Let Kinetic Gal share some of her ideas with you!

– Sweets and candies

This is one of the simplest and easiest to prepare as birthday treats for the kids. This is a high hit on the list of party treats as kids simply love candy (admit it, even adults love chocolates and candies too!). It is one of the easiest and most affordable to purchase. This makes it a pretty common party treat, but if some effort is put into searching for the candies, it can be a good party treat too!

– Party blowers and mask

Fun stuff to have for the kids: it definitely lets the kids bring up the party's atmosphere! One thing to note though, while the kids may be really having fun with things like whistles, it might be prudent to have them distributed only after shows (if there are shows planned), as they might be noisy, consequently posing a challenge to your entertainer from entertaining the kids with his best at his show.

– Little puzzles

Kids love challenges. Having little puzzles for birthday treats let the little tots and the older ones put their mind to work and have some fun-time trying to figure out the puzzles. In fact, make use of the treats for games too, and have a competition of solving the puzzles in the shortest time possible during your party.

– Tattoos and Stickers

Of course, tattoos here refer to the temporary tattoos that you can find in many novelty shops nowadays. Depending on your party theme, you can have scary real looking tattoos, pixie tattoos, cartoon tattoos, so on and so far. Stickers are also an alternative that you can consider.

BALLOON DECORATIONS

Kids are always fascinated by balloons. They are fascinated by the colours, and the fact that balloons float (though some do not). As it is, not just kids love balloons event; the truth is adults do too. Here are some tips to which kind of balloons to use for your party:

1. The types of balloons that one can use for decoration ranges from the most basic 10"/18" round balloons, to various shaped balloons and aluminium foil balloons and so on and so forth. Most times, the round balloons are mixed with a mixture of a few foil balloons (for the backdrop with happy birthday wordings). 260 balloons are mostly used for balloon sculpturing, so if you want to have loads of balloons for the kids to take and play with, that kind of balloon would be suitable.

2. Sometimes, you have little kids and toddlers at the party, and they would want balloons too. If that is the case, prepare several foil balloons that can be easily blown up but will not burst nor deflate easily. These balloons are easily available at party supply stores, and are safe balloons for the young kids.

Tip 1 applies more to helium balloons, but the rest can apply to non-helium balloons.

Some generic things to take note:

For decorations with non-helium balloons, ribbons and strings would be your best friends. Get creative with the ribbons and make full use of low pillars, vents, etc. from the ceiling. Tying ribbons across and using these ribbons to hang the balloons actually gives the illusion of floating balloons. Hang your balloons at curtains, pillars, doors, etc.. Sometimes, you may want also, to use double sided tape instead of ribbons, but do be careful of the walls and wallpaper as they sometimes leave marks.

TIP 1: LET THEM LOOSE.

For some very basic balloon decorations, helium balloons are the best. If you are looking at doing the balloon decorations yourself, you do not really need to crack your head over where to find helium balloons. Locally, if you need just a small bunch of helium balloons, spotlight at Plaza Singapura actually sells the helium tubs you need for blowing up helium balloons. If you really wish to do the balloon decorations yourself, mixing some helium balloons with non-helium ones would be the most cost-effective and still, impressive decorations you can have!

TIP 2: GO BONKERS WITH COLOURS

Pick your colours wisely. For younger children's birthday parties (1-5years), a wide variety of colours are fine. If you are going with a themed party, try to go for the balloons that match that theme. There are pre-printed balloons that say "Happy Birthday". These are great as well, as they are usually already coloured to the theme, so these can be great to incorporate with coloured balloons around the room.

TIP 3: PLACE THEM RIGHT

Hang the balloons in the right spots. If you are just blowing them up and hanging them, try to find the right spots around the room(s) to place them so they are not in the way or blocking anyone's view. Corners of windows or doors, on top of furniture, and higher up on walls are great places to hang them.

TIP 4: BUNCH THEM TOGETHER

Use bunches of balloons to decorate. Try to do the balloons in groups of four or five. It is always better to hang balloons in a bunch because it makes more of an impact. This will help create a better party atmosphere around the room. Ribbons can also be hung from under the balloons to help create an even more unique party feel!

No matter what kind of party you are throwing, balloons are always a great way to go. And afterwards, you know that you will have entertainment for hours trying to find fun ways to pop them! So have fun picking out your coloured balloons for your next party and remember these tips and ideas when you are hanging them around the party room.

As with most decorations and party games, one of the most important things to the decorations would be creativity! You are only limited by your creativity! So unleash your creativity, have fun designing the decorations (with your child even, if you wish!).

THEMING THE BIRTHDAY PARTY

I usually get asked this question a lot – is it always necessary to theme a birthday party? The answer is "Yes!", but not necessarily in the way that you think. Theming of the birthday party can mean the decision to go with a party-type (dance theme) and not always a story or character-based theme.

Theming the birthday party allows you to know what direction to go for the birthday party. Besides, it also makes it easier to make decisions on what to do and activities to plan. Depending on your theme, decorations may come into play, and if so, you would need to budget and plan in advance.

One important point when it comes to theme parties: Always adopt a holistic approach when planning a theme party. The theme only comes about when different elements come together to create a synergistic effect and experience!

SCIENCE THEMED BIRTHDAY PARTY

Studies may be boring to some but definitely not all kids find science boring. In fact, if your kids like science, planning a science themed party may be a great idea. Science themed party can be a great hoot and fun to plan too! A science student myself, I love science parties. So here are just some quirky and fun ideas.

Invitations

For invitations, you can use some lemon juice on paper. It is after all a science principle that you are using for the invitations! It can be pretty cool for the kids to try to get the words of the invitation only after heating the invitations. If you think that heating of the invitation may be dangerous (adult supervision is advised!), another thing to consider is the writing of the invitation in ultraviolet ink. Send the invitations together with the ultraviolet pen (and light included) and let the kids have fun with the UV pen as well. Of course, remember to specify in the invitation that it is a science themed party and remind everyone to come in their craziest scientist costume!

DECORATIONS

For a science themed party, hanging up decorations would be difficult to theme to science. However, it is possible to make the place a lot more 'science-lab' like, with crazy meters hanging around. One of the more fun things to do for a science themed party would be the cups and plates for food. Instead of regular cups and plates, have some plastic conical flask with a nice capillary tube (straw!) for drinks. Use petri-dish like plates (or even test tubes!) for your jellies and agars! Some of these items can be found in novelty stores and can be fun to have.

ENTERTAINMENT

For science themed entertainment, we can have some fun science 'experiments'. Have a goo-making competition! Much like how Harry Potter does his brewery of his magic potions, the children attending the party can have 'science potion classes'. How to conduct this 'science competition' is really up to you. If you are fretting because you have no idea of how and what to use, simply do a quick search online and you will find a lot of resources with regards to this.

Of course, even though it is a science themed party, not all entertainment must be so 'experiment' oriented. Remember the science fiction novel Frankenstein? For the party, have a competition with some materials provided for the kids (split into groups) to come up with a best looking Frankenstein! A costume competition is always a hit with the kids, and this is just a little twist on the traditional dress-up competition.

CIRCUS THEMED PARTY

Circus themed party can be an extremely fun party for kids who belong to the more hyperactive type as well as those who are interested in circus arts. Why not plan a circus themed party for your kid whose birthday party is just round the corner.

DRESSING UP FOR THE OCCASION

Since it is a circus themed party, why not have everyone invited to dress up as different characters that one can find in a circus? Have everyone invited to dress up for the party and have your child dressed up as the ring master (since he/she is the birthday child). This will definitely add to the atmosphere of the party. To make it fun, it would be nice to have free gifts of clown nose to all who arrives. This can double up as a doo gift too.

DECORATIONS

For decorations, thinking along the line of circuses, it would be really cool if you have enough space to create a circus tent like tentage. It may not be exactly a circus tent, but it could be something along the lines of round seating, or partial round seating with a centre stage. Put in colourful balloons, pseudo-real posters of performers (make up some funny ones with your birthday kid's photo, or even your own photos) all around the tentage for a real circus, and create carnival-like atmosphere.

PARTY BAGS

For a circus themed party, consider having party bags with face painting kits, or small finger animal puppets. Hats that are juggler or clown-like are also hot favourites. Also, consider putting some light sticks in the bag for the kids to have some fun with some glow-in-the dark action at night too.

GAMES AND ENTERTAINMENT

For games, there could be a face painting competition (or you could have a real face painter at the party) and best dressed competition. You can have an Animal's Charade (charade but only with animals you find in circuses), Monkey Hear Monkey Do (actually a tweaked version of Simon Says) and even the traditional Pin the Donkey's Tail. You could rent a candy floss machine too for the day, and that would really add to the atmosphere. As for entertainment, you can always look for jugglers, clowns or even contortionists. However, do note that while clowns are a standard at circuses, some young kids are in fact, scared of clowns, so jugglers who can do magic (actually, just like yours truly :P) would be a great option.

Whatever it is, just remember, the birthday party is a great way for the kid to have fun (and for you too), so the best thing is to enjoy the whole process and have fun planning the party.

MAGIC THEMED PARTY

With the recent craze of Harry Potter series, it is little surprise that some children would like their birthday party to be magic themed. Some ideas you can draw from for a magic themed party includes shows like: Harry Potter, Lord of the Rings, Charmed, Sabrina the Teenage Witch, and also, magicians like David Copperfield, David Blaine, Criss Angel and so forth.

To organize a great magic themed party, there are many elements to take care of. The various elements include: Invitational cards, door gifts, party decoration and entertainment. It sounds like quite a lot, isn't it? Fret not; here are some tips to organizing a great magic themed party for you.

INVITATIONAL CARDS

For invitational cards, you can let your creativity get to work to make some magic-themed cards. Why use the old dreary cards that you can buy outside, when you can make yours, specially themed, together with your child? Get your child to join in the fun by allowing him/her to make the cards together. Remember the Marauder's Map in Harry Potter? Well, you can make your invitation cards like these, simply by making your cards in a scroll form. Crumple the paper (parchment!) beforehand and then scorch the sides to make it look like a scroll, before writing your invitation.

You can also make a 'magic' invitation card that will only show its magic words when heated. Cut out the paper in different shapes and write your invitation in lemon ink. The invitation will only appear when it is heated up – but do remember to include instructions on how to read your magic invitation.

Magic = stars and moon. Hence, for your invitation, you can also use potato prints to print on your invitation cards before writing your invitations. Simply cut your potato (uncooked) to the shape you want (Star or moon) and use poster colours to print the shapes on your invitation cards.

Remember to include all relevant details in your invitation cards and state explicitly if you wish your child's friend to come in magic costumes so they can all join in the fun of costume dressing.

DOOR GIFTS

Fantastic door gifts you can gift to the friends of your child attending the party include anything that is magic themed! Anything that would go well with the costumes is a good idea for door gifts. For example, you can have wands, Harry Potter spectacles, scar tattoo (on the forehead!), wizard hats and so on. You can choose to buy the door gifts or make them yourself. They do not have to be very difficult – Harry Potter Spectacles can be made from pipe cleaners, wizards hats from paper cones (just stick some stars and moons on the hat!) and so on.

You can also have a mini-magic set that teaches the children some simple magic tricks, for door gifts. Alternatively, you do not need to give a magic set each, but various simple effects and tricks for the children. You can also ask your local magic shop for ideas and recommendations. These magic shops (physical or online) should be able to offer bulk discount too, so you can get fantastic door gifts without spending too much money and effort.

PARTY DECORATIONS

Party decorations set the mood and surroundings for the party, and so is exceptionally important for ANY themed party – magic themed party included. Balloons are something that all children love, and they are the 'generic' decorations. Therefore, you can use them for the magic themed party decorations too. Simply request that the balloons be colour themed to the theme of your party. For magic theme, gold, black and silver balloons would be great colours for your party.

Magic is always associated with playing cards so why not use playing cards for decorations too? Normal poker sized playing cards can be stuck on the backs of the chair (Ace of Spade for the birthday child of course) and the children can also have fun choosing the 'card-chair' they wish to sit on. In fact these cards can double up for lucky draw too. You can prepare another deck beforehand to draw the lucky winner – he/she must be sitting at the chair with the same card. For the surrounding decorations, you can buy Jumbo Poker Cards (available in magic stores) to stick on the wall. These cards are huge in size and make a good decoration.

Instead of the usual streamers, you can make gold star shapes from gold colour pipe cleaners. Simply string them up using some raffia string, and hang them up wherever you wish. You may also wish to create mood lighting using candles. However, since fire is quite a hazard – especially when there are children around, you can use electric fire lamps instead. Flickering light gives the venue a semi-spooky and mysterious feel, much like the wizarding world. And of course, if the magic theme is leaned towards the wizarding world, feel free to stand a few brooms labelled Nimbus 2000 around in your venue and so on.

ENTERTAINMENT

Simple entertainment that would fit the bill for the magic party includes: the best dressed wizard/ magician/witch competition and broom racing and even, a magic competition! You can write in your invitation cards beforehand that each child should come for the party with a magic trick (simple one) prepared. Have a half-an-hour competition where each child comes up to perform a simple effect. The best magician wins a prize!

Of course, since you are holding a magic themed party, what more suitable entertainment could there be than hiring a magician for your party? In fact, if your party includes the adults, you can even hire close-up and walk-around magicians to let everyone (adults included) enjoy the magic up close and personal. You can let the children experience the magic show and even request the magician to make your child the magic star of the show!

CARTOON THEMED PARTY

Cartoon is the ONE universal thing that all kids have watched, be it the 'older' Mickey Mouse, to the Power Puff Girls, Power Rangers, Ben10, so on and so forth. Thus, if your kids love cartoons, why not have a cartoon themed party for his or her birthday? Here are some ideas for the various aspects of the party for a cartoon theme.

INVITATIONS

Invitations are simple enough. There are so many party shops with cartoon-characters printed invitations. If you want to save trouble, these are your best bets. Simply head down to the party supplies store and check with them if they have your kid's favourite cartoon-character invitation cards in stock. If you want to make the cards yourself, you can also do that. One simple way is to buy stickers of your kid's favourite cartoon character. You can then print out generic invitations and stick the stickers on the cards. Of course, you can get your kid involved by letting him/her help out with the invitation cards as well.

If this is a dress up party, remember to write in your invitation cards that everyone is invited to come dressed up as their favourite cartoon characters. Adults can be part of it too! Simply state in your cards to request parents to come dressed up as well – it will be great fun for all the kids to see their parents in costumes too. To make it more fun, let everyone know that there will be a competition for the person who looks most alike to the cartoon character he/she is dressing up as.

DECORATIONS

Balloons, posters and utensils are great for decorations. Cartoon themed printed aluminium balloons are the most easily found, and there should be no problems finding those. Another great thing about these balloons is that you can simply give out the balloons after the party. You would be hard-pressed to find even one kid who doesn't want one. You can also find printed utensils with the relevant cartoon in party supplies store easily too. These naturally act as decorations if they are laid out nicely on the table.

GAMES AND ENTERTAINMENT

For games, you can have say 'Robin Hood Archery Contest' using toy bow and arrows. Simply have different game stations set up according to different cartoon themes. It could be the 'Flintstone Bowling Lane', "Transformer – Build a car station" and so on and so forth. You can also have a pre-party entertainment for kids who arrive early, playing different cartoons. Put your creativity to use and let it all flow. Of course, as mentioned before, remember to have a most look-alike (to the cartoon character) competition for the children who did take the efforts to dress up. As for entertainment, you can look for licensed cartoon characters.

DANCE AND MUSIC THEMED PARTY

Do your kids love dance and music? Most kids do, and depending on the age group, the dance and music might be slightly different.

A younger age child may go with Hi-Five, while older children may go for a more child friendly disco type music.

INVITATIONS AND COSTUMES

First and foremost, for the party, try to decide if it should be a generic music/dance party or if you want it to be specifically (for example) a 'High School Musical' Party. Having decided on that, you can then send out the invitations and invite the friends and relatives to come for the party, dressed up accordingly. 'High School Musical' invitation cards are also easily found in most stores that sell party items, so you can get that if you wish. If it is a 'High School Musical' Party, you can also have all the invited kids come in cheerleader or basketball player costumes. Alternatively, have them come in dance related costumes like ballerina costumes and such.

DOOR GIFTS AND PARTY BAGS

For a music/dance themed party, a great door gift could be pom-poms for the girls and dance batons for the guys. Alternatively, you can have microphone key chains and keychain ballerinas as door gifts. For party bags, it would be extremely easy to get High School Musical related party bags. These stationeries are widely available in stores. If you want, you can buy different items separately and package them as party bags.

ENTERTAINMENT

Pre-party entertainment for a music/dance party is actually extremely wide in selection. If you happen to have a karaoke system set, that would be great for the kids as well. You would however, need an adult to ensure that there is someone who can control the songs for the kids. Some may squabble over who takes the mic, and if that happens, switch to a mass sing-along instead.

Another great idea if you happen to have the PlayStation is to actually borrow the Dance Dance Revolution game from someone. Have it set up for play in the hall and give out 'result sheets' to the kids. They can take turn to play the game and the person with the highest score wins a prize at the end of the party.

Of course, this being the dance/music party, you could simply choose an easier way (less things to oversee) out by just playing the High School Musical DVD on your TV as a preshow and warm-up entertainment. Kids love repetition (if they like the item), so even if most of them have seen it before, they would still love to see it again.

Besides the party magician/juggler/ventriloquist that you can hire for the party, consider also having a music band for the party. You can source for the bands from junior colleges and universities. Most of these have a decent standard and are still pretty affordable.

GAMES

For games, you can ask the entertainer whom you have hired (if you decide to) to have music/dance related games. If you prefer to do it yourself, you can have games such as guess the song, or musical chairs/statues. For musical chairs, children tend to rush and in the process often get injured. To avoid that, you can switch to having coloured pieces of paper on the ground. Instead of 'fighting' for the seats, have them stand on the piece of paper when the music stops. Making them stand still on the paper when the music is stopped will cut injuries to a minimal. Of course, do not forget to have a prize for the winners of each game and the best-dressed person.

PUPPET THEMED PARTY

While the recent new anime and cartoon series have invaded the children's TV programs, shows like Sesame Street and Muppets are still core programmes children watch as they grow up. Indeed, it is rare that any child have not watched or heard of Sesame Street and/or Muppets before.

While that is so, there are few parties in Singapore that are puppet themed. Hence, if you want something novel and fun for your children's birthday party, why not – A puppet themed party??

DECORATION IDEAS

Since this is going to be a puppet themed party, you can make use of any famous puppet cartoon or even shows that make use of puppets for decoration ideas. You can use famous ones such as: Sesame Street or Muppets. For example, you could go online to print pictures of famous puppet characters like Elmo and so on to stick on the wall. Using the freely available pictures from the internet, you could print banners and the likes easily. Of course, if you wish, you can allow your child to choose his/her favourite character as the theme – it is after all his/her special day!

Balloons are a must for all parties, so for puppet themed parties, you could get Sesame Street helium aluminium balloons which are easily available at most party supply stores. You can look for balloon decorators who can make balloon characters that can stand at the door to welcome your guests. Of course, these balloon characters will be famous puppets from children shows.

If there is a table setting, you can make things more fun, by having simple sock puppets on each child's cup. Simply invert each cup and pull a sock puppet over the cups. The puppet need not be very complicated. All you will need is a lot of socks (new socks are recommended – the parents may not be happy with the kids getting old sock puppets) and of course, some plastic eyes that can be bought at art stores. You can get bright and colourful socks from night market and simply stick on a pair of eyes for each of the socks. This makes a good decoration at the table and the kids can bring the puppet home after the party too.

DOOR GIFT IDEAS

For door gifts, you could give each child that attends your party a puppet making kits. Kits like these for children are commercially available and are pretty affordable and have all the items needed for making a nice hand puppet. Of course, puppets do not refer to just hand puppets. Besides being cute and lovable, finger puppets are affordable as door gifts too.

Alternatively, if the setting is not table setting (as described above) you could have the sock puppets as door gifts too. In fact, the sock puppets can double up as a candy sock. Stuff the socks with candies and the little party favours that you have prepared for the children, and tie them up with pipe cleaners. Not only do they have a candy goody bag, they also have a sock puppet to play with.

MUSIC IDEAS

Since you are having a party, music must be a given. For a puppet themed party, consider having Sesame Street songs for the background music instead of the traditional music. Of course, that can also be extended to the birthday song. Birthday song that is sung by the Muppets can be easily found, so you can use that for the party as well.

ENTERTAINMENT

For entertainment, you could have a puppet making station. If you have given a puppet kit for the children as a door gift, encourage them to open their kit and have fun doing up their puppets. All you need is a table, some chairs, scissors, glue, wool (for puppet hair), pipe cleaners, straws and anything that they wish for the puppet, and your puppet station is ready.

Of course, to make it more fun, announce a 'puppet-making contest' and the kids will be gearing to go to make the loveliest puppets. You can even have different categories for your puppet competition such as: 'Cutest Puppet', 'Most Scary-Looking Puppet' and so on and so forth.

You can also have some recordings of the famous puppet voices from the shows that the children are familiar with, for the children to have a 'Guess Which Puppet" game. Alternatively, source for songs from various puppet shows and have the children guess which show the song comes from.

FAIRY TALE THEMED PARTY

Almost all children grow up reading and listening to fairy tales. Boys love to act like the knights and princes, and girls – princesses! It is hence, no big surprise that a fairy-tale theme is one of the most popular choices for birthday party themes around. It can be cost efficient, but will require some time and effort.

PARTY INVITATIONS

For a fairy-tale themed party invitation, you can make the invitation cards like a decree or scroll. Use a cream-coloured texture paper for best effect. Handprint the text of the invitation with a fountain pen or print it out on your computer, using an old-English calligraphy font. To attain the look of an old scroll, simply crumple the paper and scorch the paper sides. Tear the paper sides before scorching to give it a 'scroll-look', but be careful when handling fire!

For fairy-tale themed parties, the kids can dress up to fit the theme. Your invitation should state this explicitly so that the invited children can do so. (You might want to have simply costume accessories such as hats/ helmets/ tiaras/ fairy wings etc. just in case some kids are not in costume.)

The invitation itself should be written in a fun way too, but do remember to put in all the relevant details including: date, time (duration), venue, RSVP date and contact details.

DOOR GIFTS/ PARTY BAGS

Some door gifts or party bags you can consider for a fairy-tale themed party include: plastic tiaras, wands, king/prince crowns, toy swords and shields, pirate patches and pirate hats and so on (you get the idea). The items mentioned above can be bought from party shops, or if you wish to, you can make them yourself too. Tiaras and wands can be made from colourful pipe cleaners and pirate hats, and eye-patches can be made from cheap cloth. Use your child's favourite fairy-tale story or characters as inspirations or guides to make themed door gift or party bags. You can make up inexpensive little goody bags like rustic pouches, made from old cloth, filled with gold chocolate coins and trinkets. Simply cut out a square of cloth about "8 x 8", throw in the goodies and gather up the corners of the cloth, then tie them together with twine.

CAKE

Since your party is going to be a fairy-tale themed party, there is no reason why your cake shouldn't fit in the theme too. The simplest solution is to buy cakes from confectionery shops that have fairy-tale prints on the cake. However, this can be expensive.

If you wish, you can have a home-baked cake that fits the theme. Do not worry! You do not have to be a pastry chef to make a tasty cake – you can make it easily using pre-mixed cake powder available in supermarkets. To make it even more fairy-tale themed, buy icing, sweets, chocolates and use your creativity to decorate the cake. An easy cheat to make a simple cake a themed one is to buy toy figures and plant them on the cake. Ensure that the birthday child gets involved by letting him/her design or decorate his/her own cake too. This is a great chance to bond with your child in a fun way.

DECORATIONS

For a fairy-tale themed party, decorations must reflect the fairy-tale theme. One of the best decorations that can help to create a fairy-tale atmosphere is plenty of white, silver or pink nylon netting. Nylon netting can give the surroundings a dreamy and fairy-tale feel. Nylon netting is very versatile and you can secure the material on chairs, tables, pillars and even the ceiling.

Since your child is the special child for the day, you can also have a special throne for the birthday child. This throne can be easily made by modifying an inexpensive wooden chair and have it spray-painted gold and decorated with nylon netting. You can also put red satin on the seat to make it even extra special! A plush cushion will also be a nice touch.

If you don't mind the expense, fairy-tale themed party cutlery, plates and cups are very pretty and really add to the theme when the entire table is set with such themed tableware.

Balloon decorations can easily fit the fairy-tale theme. If you are using a professional decorator, they will have the expertise to theme the decorations. If you are self-decorating, the easiest way is to match balloon colours to the other decorations. Adding stickers of fairy-tale characters is an inexpensive way to theme the balloon beyond just colours.

ACTIVITIES

Think about designing your party activities like games and competitions that can incorporate a fairy-tale theme. Here are some ideas; a best-dressed fairy-tale character or most creative fairy-tale costume competition, colouring contests featuring favourite fairy-tale characters, memory games using fairy-tale playing cards, a real-life archery competition (just like in Robin Hood) with suction-cap arrows; shooting competitions with foam or suction-cap dart guns or matching shoes to the right person, ala Cinderella. The great thing about these activities is that you can organize them yourself.

If you are hiring a party entertainer, it is a good idea to look for a professional company that can customize their shows and games.

TIPS ON CHOOSING THE RIGHT ENTERTAINER FOR YOUR KID'S PARTY

Many parents have expressed concerns on what is an appropriate show for their kids. Having been in the birthday party industry for a few years now and seeing how different kids of different ages react, here are some tips on choosing the best entertainer for your kid's party.

AGE

The first thing to keep in mind is the age of your birthday child. If your child is between 1- 3 years old, you may want to keep things simple. Children of this age are unpredictable and there is no fixed formula on choosing the right entertainer for these children. On the other hand, kids aged 9 -12 consider themselves all grown up and usually scoff at what they consider "kiddy" forms of entertainment.

But if your kid is between the ages of 4 – 8, then he/she is at an age where they are old enough to understand jokes and enjoy fun-filled interactive games or activities with lots of movement. This makes hiring an entertainer for kids in this age group easier and more worthwhile for all.

So what is the best type of entertainer to choose for the different age groups? Well, here are the three most common types commonly seen at parties:

MAGICIANS

Magicians are common choices as kid's party entertainers. Kid's magicians tend to perform bright and colourful magic such as producing a huge bouquet of flowers from an empty vase or making colourful handkerchiefs appear and disappear in the blink of an eye.

The 4 -8 year olds are generally the most appreciative and participative audience. 1 – 3 year olds are too young to really comprehend magic while the 9 – 12 year olds are more interested to find out how a trick is done than enjoy the show. This is not to say that these kids will not enjoy a magic show, but rather a good kid's magician will have to tailor his show accordingly to suit children from these age groups.

JUGGLERS

Jugglers are fast becoming a popular entertainment choice at birthday parties. Their sublime juggling skills combined with entertaining routines make them a hit not just with the kids, but the whole family.

Some jugglers also involve the audience in their routines, making the show audience participative and fun for the whole family. It is also not uncommon to see jugglers who combine elements of magic into their show as well.

As with magic shows, juggling shows require the audience to appreciate the skill that the performer is exhibiting. Younger children may not fully understand or realise a juggler's skill while older kids may tend to get bored after a while seeing the same performer attempt to juggle different things. However a good performer will be able to make his routines entertaining enough and engaging enough to suit most kids of different ages.

PUPPETEERS/ VENTRILOQUISTS

Puppets add an extra dimension of fun to any party. Kids love to see a funny looking puppet animal telling stories and cracking jokes. Puppets also make the entire show look bigger as it appears that there is a cast of performers rather than just one performer doing the show. This is one of the main reasons ventriloquist shows are a hit at parties.

Younger kids will be captivated by brightly coloured talking puppets while older kids will be able to appreciate the jokes and interact with the puppets. A ventriloquism puppet show is something that can be a fun for the whole family.

So it really depends on which and what type of entertainers you would like for your kid's party!

WORKING WITH BIRTHDAY PARTY PROFESSIONALS

You might be wondering what this section is doing in this book, given that this is meant to be a DIY Stress-free Party Handbook. Well, there are many times when this option might actually be the best option, given the conditions of the party. One might want to consider DIY-theming decorations, cakes, games and activities, and still engage a show (magic/ science/ balloon/ story-teller). This helps to take the edge of organizing a party.

Here are some tips on engaging the right birthday party professionals:

1. Before engaging the company, read through the website (blog would be even better). Does the professional write well? Call me a snob, but I believe that professionals in the field need to speak and write well, since they interact with our children.
2. Get some testimonials if possible. The best form of referrals (at least in the birthday party line) is from friends and families.
3. Call them in advance. One month is usually sufficient notice, but really popular professionals can get booked up fast. In the past, I have been booked for more than 3 shows in one single day on a regular basis.
4. Understand their requirements. Whilst they are professionals, there is little they can do if the basic requirements are not provided for. Most times, requirements are as simple as a power socket, a dedicated space for performance and for the children to gather and seat.

Most professionals will offer help when it comes to the timing of show & games. The priority for the professional is to ensure that everyone enjoys the party; especially the birthday child. However, do let the professional know if there is any delicate situations that should be highlighted and avoided before the party starts. Many times, as part of the package, they also host the birthday cake cutting. Do check in advance whether that is the case.

At the end of all, do offer the professional a drink. A glass of water is usually much appreciated.

END OF PARTY

The end of the party is just as important as the start! Before the guests leave and the clean-up begin, it's a nice gesture to have the birthday child thank the guests for coming to the party. If any party favours have been prepared, this is the right time for thank-you and the giving away of the favours.

Wrapping up the party can be quite a big chore with all the clean-up so be sure to communicate early to any friends or family member on the help needed to clean-up!

When all is done, it's just time to kick everything off… and maybe then, it might be the right time for the adult after party! After all, it is time to give yourself a big pat on the back for a wonderful birthday party planned and carried out!